BUILDINGS IN GREECE AND ROME

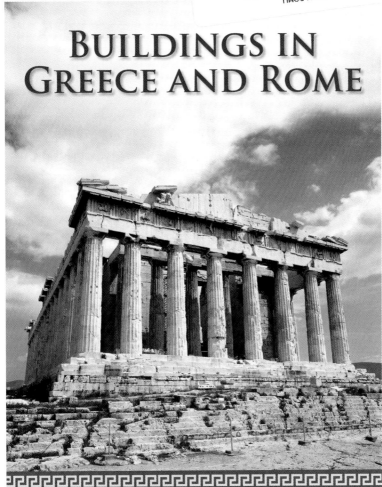

BY TAMMY ZAMBO

PEARSON
Scott
Foresman

Editorial Offices: Glenview, Illinois • Parsippany, New Jersey • New York, New York

Sales Offices: Needham, Massachusetts • Duluth, Georgia • Glenview, Illinois
Coppell, Texas • Ontario, California • Mesa, Arizona

Greek and Roman Achievements

Many aspects of life in ancient Greece and Rome still affect our lives today. For example, the United States government is a **democracy**, or a government by the people. Democracy is an idea that was first developed in ancient Greece. In addition, many modern languages are based on Latin, which was the language spoken in ancient Rome.

The achievements of ancient Greece and Rome can also be seen today in the **architecture** of buildings all over the world. Architecture is the art and science of designing and constructing buildings. The way people lived in ancient Greece and Rome affected their architecture. In turn, their architecture affected the way they lived.

Columns and Capitals

Many buildings in ancient Greece and Rome had tall columns that decorated and held up the buildings. Many columns were carved with vertical lines called *flutes*. At the top of every column was a part called a *capital*. There were three styles of capitals.

The Doric style was simple, with thick columns and plain capitals.

Greek Temples

The ancient Greeks worshipped many gods and goddesses. They built a temple for each one. The most important temple in the city of Athens was the Parthenon. It was built on the Acropolis, the highest hill in the city. Many other temples were also built on the Acropolis. The Parthenon was dedicated to Athena, the goddess of war, wisdom, and crafts. Greeks also believed Athena was the guardian of Athens, and they named the city for her.

Greek temples were not used in the same way as today's churches, synagogues, or mosques. The Greeks believed that their gods and goddesses visited the earth from time to time, and the temples were their houses during their visits. People visited the temples only to ask a god or goddess for protection, or on festival days. Sometimes they offered food or a small token as a gift at an altar outside the temple.

The Ionic style was elegant, with thinner columns and curl-shaped decorations on the capitals.

The Corinthian style was more popular with the Romans than with the Greeks. It was even fancier, and its capitals were decorated with a leafy pattern.

Athena's House

Like other temples, the Parthenon was considered a house. This house belonged to Athena. The outer part of the temple was a "porch" with a row of Doric columns around all four sides. Inside this row at each end of the temple, a shorter row of columns appeared. Next was the *cella* (SEL-eh), an inner chamber with four walls made of stone blocks with an entrance at each end. The *cella* was divided into two rooms. The main room held a wooden statue of Athena that stood 40 feet (12 meters) high and was covered with more than a ton of ivory and gold. The smaller room, in the back of the temple, contained other statues, jewels, and vases that city-states in the Delian League paid to Athens.

The Parthenon was especially important each summer, when a festival was held for Athena's birthday. This festival was called the Panathenaea (pan-AH-thee-NAH-ay-ah). It was the largest festival in Athens, and most of the people in the city took part in it.

One major part of the Panathenaea was a long parade of people and animals through the streets of Athens. The parade ended at the Parthenon, where a ritual to honor Athena was held at an outdoor altar. The Greeks designed the Acropolis with a lot of open space around the Parthenon so that large crowds like these would not disturb the gods and goddesses inside the temples.

The Parthenon was built between 447 and about 432 B.C.

The Greeks' Houses

The Greeks lived in houses of all sizes. Most houses had a central courtyard with rooms on at least three sides. Some houses also had an upper floor of rooms. The rooms usually had only small windows with wooden shutters and no glass. Baked clay tiles covered the roof.

The Greeks built their houses so that the courtyard was shaded and cool during the hot months of the year. The courtyard was a gathering place for the family. The house also had an indoor altar, where the family would worship the gods and goddesses.

If a house was large enough, the upstairs rooms were often used only by women and the downstairs rooms were used only by men. One important room was the *andron*, or dining room, where the man of the house would entertain male guests. The Greeks ate while lying down, so they often used dining couches rather than chairs. The *andron* included a low platform around the edges to hold several dining couches.

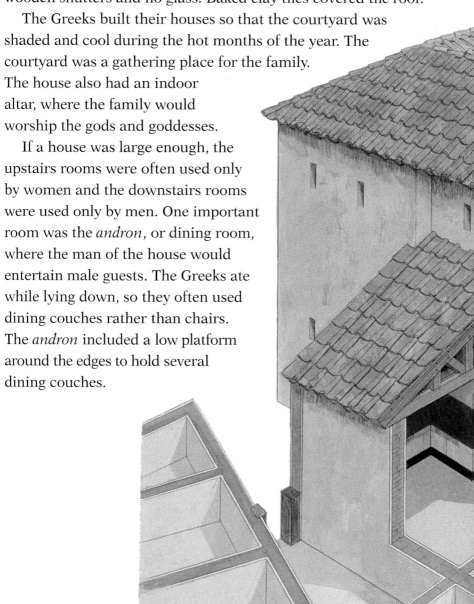

This picture shows a large house that a fairly wealthy Greek family would have lived in.

The Theater

The ancient Greeks performed the first plays and built the first theater. At the beginning, plays were performed in the **agora** in Athens, the outdoor marketplace and government center. As plays became more popular, however, more people attended and a better arrangement was needed. One side of the Acropolis sloped down perfectly to form a kind of outdoor auditorium, so the first theater was constructed there. The audience sat on wooden seats and looked down on a flat stage area. In time, seats were made out of stone and a wooden framework behind the stage was added. Actors could attach scenery to the framework and climb onto the roof for certain scenes.

The most famous Greek playwrights, or writers of plays, were Aeschylus (ES-kih-lehs), Sophocles (SOF-uh-kleez), and Euripedes (yoo-RIP-eh-deez). All of the roles in a play, including female roles, were played by men. In addition, plays included a chorus of twelve to fifteen men.

The Pantheon was built between A.D. 118 and 125.

Roman Improvements

The ancient Romans copied much of their architecture from the Greeks. For example, they borrowed the basic design of Greek temples. Romans developed **innovations**, or new ideas, as well. These innovations allowed them to design buildings in shapes and sizes that had not been built before.

The Pantheon was a temple in Rome dedicated to all the Roman gods and goddesses. Like a Greek temple, the front was a porch supported by columns. Its *cella*, however, was round instead of rectangular and had a huge dome on top. Curving surfaces such as these were a new development in architecture.

The Romans were able to build round walls and domes because they used concrete, a new building material. The Greeks had used only wood, stone, brick, and marble. The Romans mixed stone or brick with water, lime, and volcanic earth to make concrete. Concrete was much stronger than other materials, and with it the Romans built stronger arches and curved roofs called *vaults*. They combined these new features creatively to build the round *cella* and dome of the Pantheon.

Two Kinds of Homes

A wealthy family in ancient Rome lived in a home called a *domus* (DOM-uhs). The center of the domus was a hall called an *atrium* (AY-tree-uhm). The atrium usually held a shrine dedicated to the household gods. The dining room, the kitchen, and a study were attached to the atrium. Bedrooms could be located either off the atrium or on a second level of the house. A *domus* could also include rooms next to the street, which were rented out as shops. In the back of the *domus* was a garden surrounded by a row of columns called a *peristyle* (PEHR-ih-stile). A *domus* might be decorated with colorful paint and beautiful mosaics, or pictures made of small colored tiles.

Roman Religion

The Romans shared the Greeks' gods and goddesses but gave them new names. They called the king of the gods Jupiter instead of Zeus, and they called his wife Juno instead of Hera.

During the Roman Empire, Romans also worshipped their **emperor**. Romans believed in household gods called *lares* (lahr-EEZ) and *penates* (peh-NAY-teez), who watched over the home and the family's food. Each house had a shrine where the family prayed to the *lares* and *penates*.

As the empire grew, Romans conquered people from many other cultures. Those cultures had religions of their own, including Judaism and Christianity. Some Romans adopted these religions as well.

Most Romans, however, lived in crowded apartment buildings called *insulae* (IN-seh-lee). Many *insulae* were dangerous, because they were several stories high and badly built. Fires in *insulae* were common.

This is a picture of a *domus*.

A New Water System

Romans developed a very clever system of running water. They used their improved arches and new vaults to build aqueducts. These were raised structures that brought water from the mountains to the cities using gravity. The water was then collected in enormous tanks called *castella*. From the *castella*, lead pipes carried water to Roman buildings and fountains.

Most people did not have toilets at home, so many of them used latrines, or public toilets, in bathhouses. Bathhouses were also places to exercise, bathe, get a massage, snack, and relax. Some bathhouses even included a library. All of them had a well-planned system to heat water so that a visitor could choose from pools that were hot, lukewarm, or cold.

The Romans built this aqueduct near Tarragona, Rome's earliest important settlement in Spain.

The Romans' drainage system was well designed too. A web of drains under the streets took away waste water and sewage. Used bath water might flush latrines on its way through the pipes. The Romans made the most of their water in this way.

The Circus Maximus

Romans loved to attend events at a huge racetrack called the Circus Maximus. Chariot races were the most common event held there, but the circus was also used for foot races, horseback-riding shows, and fights between **gladiators**.

In the center of the Circus Maximus was a long, low structure called the *spina* (SPY-nah). It was decorated with statues, trophies, and a row of large movable egg- or dolphin-shaped counters. One of these counters was turned over at the start of each lap in a race to keep track of the number of laps.

Twelve starting gates were built into one end of the Circus Maximus. At the start of a race, teams of two, four, or more horses would spring out of the gates. Each team pulled a chariot, which was a small vehicle with two wheels. The driver was called a charioteer. The teams would race seven laps counterclockwise around the spina. Chariot races were dangerous, and charioteers were often killed or injured in crashes with other teams.

Seats in the Circus Maximus rose in staircase fashion around the track. Areas below the seats were built with vaults for strong support. Audience members climbed stairways inside these areas to reach the higher seats. The Roman senators sat in the stone seats closest to the track. The poorest spectators had to stand in the area highest up and farthest from the track. The emperor sat in a special "boxed seat" decorated with columns.

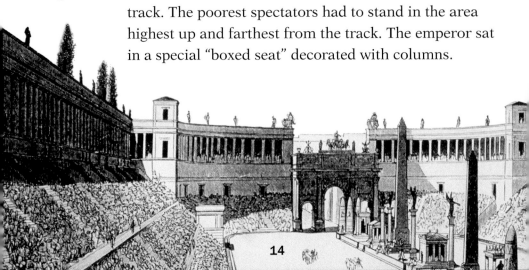

14

Skill and Imagination

In designing and building structures, the ancient Greeks and Romans displayed great skill and imagination. Both built temples to their gods and goddesses. Their houses were built to meet people's needs.

The Greeks' achievements in architecture can be seen in the Parthenon and their houses. While the Romans copied much of their architecture from the Greeks, they developed innovations of their own. One of these was concrete, which allowed the Romans to create domed structures. Romans lived in two kinds of houses, depending on their wealth. They also built aqueducts to bring water to their cities and outdoor racetracks for entertainment. How the Greeks and Romans lived affected how they built, and how they built structures affected the way they lived.

The Circus Maximus was built in the sixth century B.C. Many emperors, including Caligula and Nero, were great fans of the chariot races.

Glossary

agora the outdoor marketplace and center of
government in Athens

architecture the art and science of designing and
erecting buildings

democracy a government by the people

emperor the ruler of an empire

gladiator a professional Roman fighter

innovation something newly introduced